Spiritual High

Other Books by JOHN-ROGER

Contents

Preface

New forms of consciousness-altering, "recreational" drugs come and go. Regardless of the name or form, drugs affect your body, mind, emotions, and unconscious in powerful ways. In this book, we describe specific drugs, including alcohol, and explain how drugs affect you. You can apply this information to drugs that are not mentioned as well.

It is not our intention in this book to judge the use of drugs. In this book you will find facts and better options so you can make wise choices.

Drugs often seem to offer relief, fun, or relaxation, yet end up giving grief, disappointment, a sense of defeat, or worse. You can avoid a great deal of heartache by knowing what you are dealing with and that you have the ability to choose.

If you use drugs to experience higher levels of consciousness than what everyday life seems to offer, there are other methods that can give you more lasting and uplifting results. In addition to explaining how drugs affect your body, mind, and unconscious, we will explain spiritual exercises that you can try out for yourself. Although the power of drugs is significant, once you activate your higher nature, the thrills that they offer pale in comparison. If you are looking for adventure, then discovering, exploring, and becoming more aware of who you truly are can be one of the greatest experiences of your life.

Introduction

Drugs are all around, and having information about them can help you make wise choices about what you involve yourself in. Under medical supervision and control, the use of drugs can be a godsend. This includes drugs used in hospitals to relieve pain, or prescribed to treat or relieve symptoms of disease. Many people occasionally use drugs like aspirin, seltzer, or cold medicine, which can be very helpful. This is drug use; don't kid yourself that it's not.

We won't be talking about this type of drug use, however, except in certain cases as it relates to therapy leading to addiction. We explain some of the actions and patterns involved in drug and alcohol *abuse*, and we offer practical information that can work for you if you are open to it. Then you must check the information out for yourself.

If you don't know what drugs are really doing to your body, mind, and unconscious, this may be some eye-opening information. If you sense that these things are hurting you in some way, but you need information and options, this book is for you. If you are not using or never have used drugs, then this information may be helpful to others who come to you for guidance and support.

One reason people take drugs is because of their desire to be part of a group. Your friends or the people you want to spend time with do it, so you do too, whether or not you really want to. You go along with what is happening in order to be part of the crowd. We often hear people say, "Everybody's doing it," so they get right on that train too. God only knows where it's going to take them. One thing is certain: drugs take people off their path of spiritual fulfillment.

Young people are particularly vulnerable to this desire to fit in and be accepted. Human beings are very social creatures, but eventually you realize that you can't please everybody all the time. Regardless of your age, you are going to find out that you have to please yourself. The friends who matter so much today—and who may be the reason for your using drugs—may not even be around in a year or two. They move or go on to other things, and you are left alone with the results of your actions. *Then* what are you going to do? You'll be by yourself, and you may find that you don't seem to have much going for you. Be honest with yourself. It is common knowledge that drug addiction often leads to hospitals, jails, or death.

For those of you who are parents, this may sound like an old-fashioned cliché (and it is, but it's also still true): *It is important to give your children solid spiritual and moral training at home.* Educate your children about drugs. You don't need to say, "don't use" or "do use"; you don't need to preach or moralize. You will push your children away if you are critical or judgmental. Just say, "This is what happens." Bring out a medical book, show them the experiments, give them the information, and draw them in to talking about drugs and drug use. Educate them past this very human pattern of trying to fit in with the crowd.

There are many other reasons for getting or staying involved with drugs. The stress of everyday life is sometimes more than people feel they can handle without a drink to help them relax, a pill to get their energy up, or something just for fun. Later chapters cover the path of moving into greater and greater drug use/abuse and why that happens. Underlying many people's use of drugs is an effort to expand beyond limitations and frustrations and experience more than daily life seems to offer. The problem with using drugs in this attempt is that, ultimately, drug use actually *interferes* with our normal human capacity to experience joy, loving, and greater expression.

Certain personality traits tend towards the use of drugs. One of the main ones is the trait of *adventure*. Adventurous people will experiment just to have something to do. This trait often seems to be "the venture before the fall." If you're doing what's right and proper, you're directing yourself and you're staying out of trouble. But when you become adventurous without direction, you leave yourself open to whatever's coming your way.

Another trait that is prevalent in drug users is that of *impetuosity*. If you can learn to think before you move into action, you probably won't use drugs. You'll direct your adventures; you'll channel them and make them work for you—like the adventure of learning, painting the house, finding a new book to read, climbing a mountain, or something like this. Impetuosity gets you moving, but then you need to direct yourself into things you really want to be involved with. *Think* before you jump into your next choice, and you can start getting more of what you really want. This takes practice and builds strength.

Some people have karma, or a life path, with this area of drug abuse. But that does not excuse their involvement with drugs. It's easy to judge people who are doing drugs, but it's best not to do that. Judging doesn't change anything and more likely will shut off communication. You can help others, including your children if you are a parent, understand the pattern of drug abuse early so that when they are faced with it, they'll see what it is, confront it, and choose to bypass it. Then it is abolished and they are free to pursue other options. This can take strength and the support of loved ones who call things as they see them in a nonjudgmental way.

Finally, current research into the biochemistry and genetics of addiction clearly indicate that the predisposition to become addicted to drugs or alcohol is predetermined according to a person's genetics and therefore inheritable. The expression of addiction requires, however, the correct combination of genes and environmental exposure in much the same way that allergic reactions do. For example, an allergy to strawberries is genetically determined. If a person who possesses this allergy grows in an environment in which he/she is never exposed to strawberries, the allergic reaction of burning mouth, itching, watery eyes (and in severe cases, shortness of breath, respiratory arrest, and even death) never occurs. In much the same way, a person who possesses the genetic makeup leading toward addiction will only be able to express this addiction if this person is exposed to drugs or alcohol.

The fact that addicts are genetically different from non-addicts can be proven in a number of ways. One of the simpler ones is as follows: a normal person metabolizes alcohol to acetaldehyde and then to CO_2 and water.

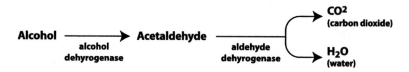

In some alcoholics, a different and unique side reaction occurs.

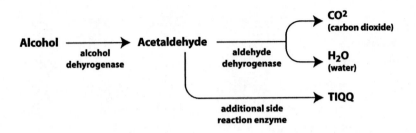

Some alcoholics possess genes that code for an additional enzyme that converts part of the acetaldehyde to TIQQ, which normal people do not have. TIQQ has the same effect on the body as heroin. TIQQ binds to the body's opiate receptors (see the chapter on heroin and opiates) and produces an addiction that can be as powerful and overwhelming as heroin addiction. These alcoholics have a completely different experience and reaction to the same drink of alcohol than a normal person. Similar biochemical variations can be demonstrated in the genetic makeup and reactions of individuals addicted to any of the various drugs. Aside from the personality and karmic reasons leading to addiction, genetics and environmental exposure also play an important role.

1

Levels of Consciousness

We come into life in this world with many levels of consciousness. You need a basic knowledge of four of them in order to understand drugs and their effects.

The *conscious self* is your everyday self that functions and relates with the physical environment; it is the one reading this book. The *high self* acts as an impersonal guardian or guide and is located about six to eight inches above your head. The *basic self* takes care of the essential, life-supporting functions of the physical body and protects the psychic centers. Your basic self is located around the area of the solar plexus or stomach, usually just above the belly button, or sometimes just below. Between the basic self and the conscious self, there is the *subconscious mind,* which records and remembers everything that happens. *Everything.*

The high self contacts the basic self, and together they work to relieve the consciousness of entities, possessions, deviant behavior, radical behavior, fantasy behavior, phantasmagoric visions, etc. The high self and the conscious self are not usually in direct contact with each other. The basic self is in direct contact with both the conscious self and the high self. Communication between the high self and conscious self is through the basic. The high self can go down to the basic self and then come up through the basic self to reach the conscious self. An important key here is that things that disturb or get locked into the subconscious can become a block to your inner flow of communication, disturbing your sense of wholeness.

When this happens, you can feel oddly disconnected from yourself or find that you think one thing and do another. You can feel as though there's more than one "you" making decisions and running the show.

Each of these levels of consciousness has a rhythm or pattern that is normal for it. Ideally, these rhythms parallel each other and flow in unison: the periods of being "up" and the periods of being "down" happen at the same time on all the levels. When this takes place naturally, you feel as though you are functioning as one unit and have a sense of being whole rather than being scattered or fragmented.

Some people have a gentle rhythm. Their ups aren't very high and their downs aren't too low; they are stable people, never really getting excited about things, but never really getting depressed either. They move along the middle path.

Then there are those who have extreme highs and lows. They get *very* excited and elated over some particular thing, and then the bottom falls out and they are deeply discouraged and depressed. The rhythms of their conscious and subconscious minds appear jagged, with higher peaks and lower valleys. Both of these patterns can be normal.

There are any number of variations between these two extremes. Everyone has normal ups and downs, and there is a security and usefulness in knowing what your personal rhythm is. When your rhythm is flowing downward, it's good to do methodical, routine work. When the rhythm starts moving up, you can become creative and accomplish a tremendous amount. As your rhythm levels off and starts going down again, you return to doing the routine things. You can learn to recognize your normal rhythms and become adept at working within them.

The subconscious mind functions in a different pattern, more like a spiral or a coiled spring. The levels of the spiral are so close together that experiences will often seem similar. Many of our blocks, frustrations, and problems reside in the subconscious mind. By definition, these things are below the conscious level, so we are not aware of them. But they are there, and in a sense, they can control us if we can't release them.

An example might be an irrational fear of water or heights.

Consciously, there may be no reason for these fears; yet when they surface, you feel helpless to do anything about them. At some previous time, you may have had a traumatic experience related to water or falling and that experience lodged itself in your subconscious mind. Each time the subconscious cycles around to that place on your spiral, you will experience that fear again. There are many examples of this type of situation. Wherever the blocks are and whatever they are related to, they stop the flow; and wherever there is a block, there will be some frustration.

In addition to having different levels of consciousness, we also come into this life with what is known as karma—those things that we must fulfill in order to grow and progress into higher consciousness. We define karma as incomplete actions from our past that need to be finished. Both the high self and the basic self know what our karmic path is and what we are to accomplish and complete. It is the basic self, however, that works directly with the conscious self to bring forward experiences and opportunities to fulfill and release our karma.

If you've been to Disneyland, you've probably seen the *Mark Twain* or *Columbia*. These big boats are like old Mississippi riverboats. You get on, and the boat goes along a waterway. No matter what happens, that boat can't go astray because it has rails underneath it guiding it through the water. It has to go along that prescribed route. Our karmic path, expressing itself first through the basic self and then the conscious self, works much like those underwater rails. Our karma sets up our path through life, and we must stay on that track. Our free will in determining our route was exercised *before* we incarnated onto this planet. That was when we set the rails in place and made the decisions about the direction of our route. Now as we go through our life, we have a lot of choices. The boat is pretty big, and we can move around on it, but the overall route of the boat remains set.

This explanation of some of our levels of consciousness has been brief, but it gives a foundation so that we can move on. Most of the effects of drugs are related to the subconscious mind and the basic self, and we will explain the physiological effects as we go.

Hallucinogenics

Mind expanding drugs such as LSD (lysergic acid diethylamide) have been abused a great deal. LSD, which is made from the ergot, or mildew, off of rye or wheat, was discovered around 1934 in Switzerland. At one time, it was produced legally for commercial use by at least one laboratory. There's also a lot of it available on the black market. Black market LSD is powerful and more dangerous than what was commercially produced because it is made with no quality control. Black market LSD is not chemically pure, and there is no way, when purchasing it, to accurately determine just what its chemical makeup is. Those who are producing and buying illegal LSD don't care about it being "safe" or predictable, as long as it will give them a "trip." Anybody with the right paraphernalia and information can make it. It can be produced in great quantity but with very little quality control.

Morning glory seeds: A hallucinogenic effect similar to LSD can also be attained by eating a large quantity of morning glory seeds. Fifty to one hundred seeds are necessary for a single effective dose. The seeds are usually ground to a powder in a coffee grinder. The powder is purified with ether or alcohol, filtered and dried, and then ingested in a mixed drink. The effect is rapid in onset and lasts eight to twelve hours.

Psilocybin (peyote, magic mushrooms, "shrooms"): Certain specific mushroom types containing psilocybins have been used for thousands of years by Native Americans in Central and South America. The mushrooms are eaten and their hallucinogenic effect occurs within 30-60 minutes and lasts for approximately six hours. Initially, anxiety and anticipation occur, followed by mental stimulation, feelings of insight, visual hallucinations, etc. Some users may seek spiritual awareness or a universal understanding through the use of the hallucinogenic plant. As with LSD, the dangers of a bad trip may develop, including frightening and horrible hallucinations, psychoses, and paranoid delusions. All hallucinogenics may be additionally dangerous if used by normal individuals with a family history of schizophrenia or other mental illness, as they may actually trigger latent psychological or mental problems.

Mescaline (peyote): Mescaline is one of the oldest psychedelics known to man. It has also been used historically in the religious ceremonies of Native Americans. Mescaline is derived from a small cactus that grows wild in the Southwestern U.S. and Northern Mexico. It is ingested in a dry form called buttons. Psychedelic effects are similar to LSD.

The dangers of using any of these hallucinogenics are similar and include "bad trips," psychosis, and the triggering of latent psychological disorders.

Effects on the Subconscious

The effects of LSD are significant. Let's say that you are going along normally; the rhythms in the levels of your consciousness are flowing pretty much in unison. Then at some point, you take LSD or some other form of psychedelic, and you "trip." The usual LSD trip lasts between nine and fifteen hours. During this time, your system stops its normal pattern and moves off its customary path. You go up real high, and when you're up, because of the abnormally rapid acceleration rate, you reach into a "higher consciousness." You do; there's no question about that at all. But when you come back down, you have to enter into a compensatory pattern; you have to balance the action. There are people who aren't constitutionally able to handle these rapid shifts in the functioning of their mind and body, and they may become psychologically disturbed. But the person who can sustain this action may like it and take LSD again to try to repeat the experience.

Let's go back to the analogy of the Disneyland riverboat. The effect of taking drugs (and this includes LSD, DMT, speed, downers, uppers, marijuana—*all* of them) or getting drunk on alcohol can be compared to the effect of someone going to Disneyland and destroying about twenty feet of that underwater railing. LSD does this rapidly; some of the others like marijuana take a little longer. Regardless, the end result is that an area of that foundation and support is gone. When the boat comes to this point, it will drift off the rail and be without direction in the water. The captain might spin the wheel, but it won't do much good. He might consider, "What will I do with my life and the lives of all these people with me?" He might be lucky and bump back onto the railing later, but that's really an outside chance. Without direction, he'll be drifting with the current, and he'd probably crash into the shore before too long.

When you have taken drugs, you have blown a hole in the pattern of your subconscious mind; the railing has been ripped up. You have really done a number on yourself, and you then go on a different path. You have lost your ability to steer yourself; you've lost all the connections with what's going on. You may find yourself drifting, floundering, and splitting off more and more from your conscious self and your conscious direction. If you have a very strong conscious self and if your conscious direction is strong, you may be able to sustain and continue in that direction for quite some time. There are people who have taken hundreds of acid trips and are still functioning fairly well on the conscious level. But they are the exceptions and *not the rule.*

As you split off more and more from your conscious self, a number of things may take place. Because the subconscious mind works in a spiral pattern, each time it cycles around to the area where the "trip" took place, it will trip again, often called having "flashbacks." Most of the time, these are not nice experiences, and you usually feel weird and upset because you can't handle what's happening. You can't control this action; it pulls you back into that pattern and you can feel extremely lost and without direction.

When this flashback experience happens, you may even contemplate suicide or other self-destructive actions. You may also become so frightened that you lock yourself into a fear pattern and become paranoid: "People are out to get me. I wonder if they're talking about me. They're taking advantage of me. I have to watch out for the police, etc." The subconscious mind and the emotions that it controls are no longer in contact with the conscious mind and the reality of the environment, and these patterns of paranoia can take place.

Another possibility is that the subconscious mind can move into a schizophrenic pattern, with extreme highs and lows in a totally erratic, unpredictable pattern. People affected in this way may or may not be able to function outside of a mental institution.

A third possibility is that you might become withdrawn; you may back away from reality and find another reality, which is probably lower than your original one. If this happens, you will probably also end up in a mental institution.

Many people are vegetating in mental institutions right now because of the effects of these drugs. It was their own action, their own choices that allowed these things to happen. They could have chosen something else. They can break out of this and assume the normal patterns of their consciousness again, but it's difficult.

Effects on the Physical Body

Drugs also affect the physical body. There are several interesting physiological reactions to look at. We have what is called a natural brain barrier, which helps us distinguish between reality and illusion. When drugs come into the blood stream, they chemically destroy the natural brain barrier. When this screening device is gone, the person hallucinates and sees all sorts of weird things in the air. Sometimes they tap into the lower astral realm (*see glossary*), which can be rather terrifying. Other people have tapped pretty high in the astral realm, and they say, "This is it! I've found God." Well, they found one of the gods, but it's one who will make sure they come back and do things over again.

Medical research into the genetic effects of LSD is, at best, inconclusive. The basic self is the one that brings in the karmic path of children and it also protects. But if its action is destroyed, it cannot fulfill its function, and a mutation of some kind or another usually takes place.

The "thalidomide children," by the way, were a different process. Most of these children had no karma. They came in and sacrificed themselves to teach the parents a lesson of responsibility. Most of them were extremely advanced Souls who came here to be of service to one or two people. That's a tremendous sacrifice; they really knew what the love factor was and were willing to demonstrate it.

Drugs also affect your nervous system. The nerves of the body are connected to one another in an interesting way. Each nerve is separated from the next by a small space called a synapse. Extending part way into this space are tiny fibrous extensions called axons and dendrites. And filling this space is an acid called acetylcholine (which acts as a conductor for the nerve impulse) and an enzyme that inhibits the production of acetylcholine. Together, these two chemicals act as a natural barrier for the nerve impulses, allowing only those impulses to proceed to the brain that are strong enough to bridge the synapse. Thus, when these two chemicals are in the correct balance, they foster a selectivity that ensures that only the "important" signals from a nerve will reach the brain.

When an impulse is sent through a nerve, it comes to the synapse, and if it is strong enough to jump the barrier between the nerves, the message or impulse goes on. If the nerve energy is not sufficient to arc across the synapse, it backs up to a sort of reverberating circuit and travels around the circuit until it either dies out or picks up enough energy to again shoot to the end of the nerve, arc across the threshold, and move to the next nerve. Some people have a greater space between the nerves than others, and the nerve impulse must be stronger for them to be aware of it. Some who are more sensitive will have a lesser space and their awareness may be much more subtle and fine. We might call them the natural psychics.

When you take LSD or some other drugs, the enzyme inhibitor of acetylcholine is wiped out and the impulses seem to go straight across. Thus, with the impulse-conducting acetylcholine filling the synapse (because its production is not being regulated), almost *all* nerve impulses are carried to the brain; nothing is blocked as it would be normally.

Also, a portion of the brain stem called the *reticular activating system* is responsible for filtering out nonessential sensory input (for example, the feeling of the shirt on your back) and only allowing important sensory input into the higher senses of consciousness (for example, the sounds of the conversation you are having or the images of the words on the page as you read this). Certain drugs inhibit the reticular activating system's ability to filter out nonessential sensory information and cause an overload of sensory stimuli to reach the higher brain centers. You think you're having a wonderful vision, and it is only that there is no restriction on your nerves and the energy is moving straight across. You're out of control. Someone turns on a light, and you think the light has gone clear through you, and the colors seem so magnificent. Someone turns on a water faucet and you think you can hear Niagara Falls. There is no discrimination and no restriction on the nerve impulses that reach your awareness. The more LSD you take, the more solid this bridging of the nerves becomes.

As this continues, you lose your discriminating values, your selectivity. Without these barriers and boundaries that are your natural brakes, you may begin disregarding your moral compass or losing track of it. It's as natural as the next step; the attitude becomes one of, "Who cares? It doesn't make any difference." You *will* perceive life differently. You will perceive everything in a different way and what you perceive as truth is what you're going to act or react to. So your life changes and everybody is saying you're weird, but you may think, "They don't know; they haven't had it."

Psychic Influences

Another possible effect of taking drugs is that of entities taking control over your body. Drugs and alcohol open the door to this taking place, and I'll go into more detail about the process with alcohol later in this book.

As we mentioned earlier, the basic self is the one that controls the psychic centers, the chakras of the body. This control is destroyed through the use of drugs. You destroy all your natural protection and leave yourself wide open for anything to come into your body. You can pull in disincarnate entities that attach to you and assume control of your body. They have every right to do this because you have abandoned your control. These entities can take you over and direct your life into any pattern that will fulfill their needs and desires. For example, if the entity was an alcoholic and is bound to the earth by its desire for alcohol, you may very well become an alcoholic, and so forth. It takes a great deal of conscious direction and fortitude of purpose to get rid of these entities once they have attached themselves to you. But it can be done when you are ready to stop the behaviors that allow them in and start building your personal strength through spiritual practices.

Pills

Downers (Benzodiazepines)

"Downers," as that term implies, take you down and are known by many street names: reds, RD's, Seconal, Nembutal, Tuinal, Trugnol, rainbows, red jackets, yellow jackets, etc. They bring you down by suppressing the central nervous system. These drugs are addictive; withdrawal symptoms are so severe that they can kill.

The technical term for the major class of downers is benzodiazepines. These include many of the most commonly physician-prescribed, addictive medications for anxiety. Examples are Ambien, Dalmane, Halcion, Klonopin, Librium, Restoril, Sonata, Valium, and Xanax. These medications are usually prescribed for anxiety, insomnia (sleeplessness), and sometimes seizures. They are generally taken in low doses over relatively long periods of time by well-meaning patients under psychiatric or general medical care.

Despite the fact that these medicines are most often legitimately prescribed to patients by duly licensed M.D.'s and psychiatrists, low dose benzodiazepine syndrome is extremely widespread and is the most powerful addictive syndrome, with the most long lasting and profoundly unpleasant withdrawal consequences. Withdrawal from these medications can include extreme anxiety, nausea, vomiting, sleeplessness, severe joint and tendon pains, tremors, seizures, and even death.

Benzodiazepine withdrawal is usually a more powerful, unpleasant, long lasting, and dangerous process than even heroin withdrawal.

Benzodiazepines are effective medicines when prescribed appropriately on a short-term basis (one to three months maximum). Research and understanding of the mechanics of addiction is still relatively new and has not yet spread adequately through the medical community. It is not at all uncommon today to find well-meaning, licensed physicians prescribing appropriate low doses of benzodiazepines to their patients on a *long-term* basis, unwittingly creating a powerful addiction with a dangerous withdrawal syndrome. We want to stress this point because this is potentially a very significant risk to people who otherwise would not deal with drug addiction.

Benzodiazepine addiction is generally not the result of shadowy, illegal, recreational drug use. It generally results from people following the medical direction of well meaning, licensed physicians treating their patients. If you are prescribed these medicines on a long-term basis (in excess of one to three months), it is important to seek a second or third medical opinion in order to protect yourself from this addictive syndrome.

An additional danger of benzodiazepines lies in their potential for overdose, especially in combination with alcohol. Both alcohol and benzodiazepines are metabolized (cleared) from the blood stream by the same enzyme system in the liver (called the cytochrome P450 system). The liver has a finite capacity to handle a benzodiazepine load *or* an alcohol load. This capacity becomes greater in persons who drink regularly or take benzodiazepines regularly. Taking benzodiazepines and alcohol together can easily overload the liver's metabolic capacity and result in temporarily toxic levels of free benzodiazepines in the blood stream, causing respiratory suppression and possibly death. Pills and alcohol are an extremely dangerous combination.

There are also many deaths that occur simply from overdosing on downers. The chance of death through the use of downers seems to be greater than with other types of drugs.

Uppers (amphetamines)

"Uppers" are amphetamines: Benzedrine (bennies), Dexedrine (dexies), methamphetamine (ecstasy), MDA, etc. Many overweight people are familiar with these because they're often used in weight control or weight loss plans. Uppers can be real terrors, making you so hyperactive inside that you'll feel like "climbing the wall." "Stay-awake pills" are about the same process as amphetamines but not quite as strong.

If you take downers or LSD, or smoke pot, you come off them slowly. You'll usually go to bed and wake up the next day with a little drug hangover and some drowsiness. By afternoon you're back up and running, and things are going pretty well. But with amphetamines, you come off in a hurry.

There is a case history that demonstrates some of the dangers of "uppers." Some years back, the fashion houses in Chicago were trying to beat each other in getting new clothing styles out to the West Coast. Flooding the California market would set the trends for the rest of the country, and the firm that placed its merchandise in California first would realize the greatest profit. Truck drivers were told, "You have to beat our competitors out to the Coast. Make the trip as fast as you can."

For the first eight hours, the drivers were doing great. They stopped for a coffee break, grabbed a cup of coffee, and popped down a pill to help them stay awake. In about thirty minutes, they were up there, driving with their eyes wide open. They developed a staring quality, and driving became just a little bit hypnotic to them. Every four or five hours, they had to stop and take another pill, and then they were usually up again and going along really well. After doing this about four times, they'd be driving down the road and suddenly fall sound asleep—and CRASH! There was no warning; they just fell asleep. Uppers let you down in a hurry once their effect starts wearing off. Students sometimes use uppers to help them cram for exams. When you wake up with your face on your books, you realize that maybe that didn't work and starting earlier might be a better approach.

Methedrine (or speed, crystal, MDA, crank) kills. A stronger form of amphetamine may be injected intravenously (into the veins) and is also frequently smoked. In both cases, it results in a short, fast trip. Amphetamine can also be snorted in a powder form resulting in a more gradual high. You go up very fast and lose not only your moral judgment but also your human values. It has an effect of distancing you from your normal sense of what is right and what is wrong, from your emotions and from any inner sense of guidance and discernment. You could kill somebody without much concern. There are many instances where someone has been beaten to death or seriously injured and speed was involved in some way.

Amphetamines can be produced cheaply in home laboratories from common household chemicals and over-the-counter products such as Pseudofed. Use of amphetamines (Ecstasy) by a pill form along with alcohol is widespread among youth attending rave parties. Sextasy, which is a combination of Viagra and Ecstasy, is also commonly used in the gay community. Ecstasy is often referred to as the "love drug" because its effects overcome normal restrictions on social behavior and may result in indiscriminate sexual activity.

Amphetamine addiction through the abuse of weight loss medications is decreasing in frequency. Because of their abuse potential, amphetamines are no longer considered medically appropriate for this purpose. Instead, the prescription of amphetamines is generally medically appropriate nowadays in the treatment of certain types of Attention Deficit Disorder (ADD) and childhood hyperactivity.

It may seem contradictory to prescribe an amphetamine stimulant to a hyperactive child. The beneficial action results from the low dose stimulation of the brain's reticular activating system. This portion of the brain stem is responsible for filtering out irrelevant sensory information and preventing it from reaching the higher brain centers. Stimulation of the reticular activating system by very low doses of appropriately prescribed amphetamine, such as Ritalin, enhances the reticular system's ability to filter out extraneous sensory input. Paradoxically, it also calms the child and allows them to more easily focus on specific tasks because of the increased filtering out of distracting sensory input.

Currently, amphetamine addiction most often results from illicit recreational use of speed, crank, crystal, or Ecstasy. The drug can be taken orally in pill or powder form, snorted or sniffed in powder form (giving an unpleasant burning sensation of the nasal membranes), smoked in a glass pipe (causing a rapid and ecstatic rush), or injected intravenously (causing an even more rapid and ecstatic rush). Initially, the effects are quite euphoric, including feelings of heightened clarity of thought, greater sense of well-being, euphoria, warm outpouring of emotion, and release of normal sexual inhibitions. Pupillary dilation, dry mouth, and sweating are common. However, continued use soon requires greater and greater dosages to reach the desired effect. The individual begins to lose weight, becomes paranoid, anxious, and irritable, and ultimately shifts focus from normal life (school, work, family, and friends) to activities relating specifically only to obtaining and using the drug. This transition may occur more rapidly and obviously in some people or more slowly and secretly in others depending on the degree of exposure, their personality, and the degree of genetic predisposition. In either case, eventually the person's major life focus becomes centered only around obtaining and using the drug.

Withdrawal from amphetamines is characterized most noticeably by irritability, isolation, weight loss, and tremor. Overdose may result in cardiac arrhythmia, seizure, stroke, heart attack, or paranoid psychosis. Long-term amphetamine addiction usually results in weight loss, psychosis, seizures, heart attack, or stroke.

Speed deteriorates the body. The places it hits first are the places where we need our energy first and foremost. The liver, which purifies the blood, will probably become damaged first. The next organ to go is usually the spleen, and after that will probably be the kidneys and gall bladder. People using speed start experiencing aches and pains in their bodies; they are often well aware that the drug use is really hurting them physically. After these organs, speed starts to affect various parts of the brain. It will usually affect the bottom part of the brain first, where our instinctive processes are centered. At this point, people think they're doing something really well and bump right into a wall. Their balance is okay; it's just that this "spinal reflex" thinking isn't working anymore. They'll hit the wall and say, "Hey, that's pretty funny!" When it starts affecting the inner ear and equilibrium, they're on their way out.

There's another drug called DMT, and although it isn't around much any more, here is the information. DMT trips last for about forty-five minutes. A lot of people took this on their lunch break, and we called them the "short trip for lunch bunch." DMT is also out to destroy the body. But the main danger is its instability. You just don't know what it's going to do.

Heroin/Opiates

The human body has naturally occurring chemicals called endorphins, which bind to specific cell surface receptors called endorphin receptors or opiate receptors. It is the binding of endorphins released by the central nervous system to the body's cell surface opiate receptors that creates a normal sense of well-being and comfort. During periods of extreme stress, such as following severe injuries, broken bones, lacerations, etc., the body releases higher levels of endorphins, which bind to the opiate receptors and decrease the mind's perception of pain to a tolerable level. This allows the individual to more easily cope with the painful emergency.

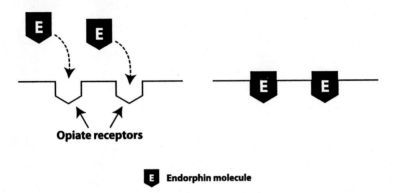

The class of drugs called opiates—including heroin, codeine, opium, Vicodin, morphine, methadone, Oxy-Contin (Percodan), Darvon, Demerol, and others—are produced from plants (e.g., heroin from poppy plant). Their chemicals are structurally similar to the body's naturally occurring endorphins and fit perfectly into the brain's cell surface opiate receptors. However, the activation of the brain's opiate receptors is much more powerful when these opiate drugs bind there than when the body's own endorphins do.

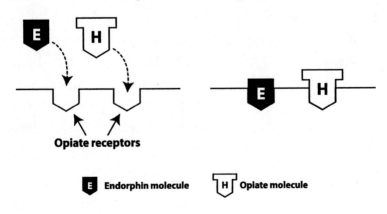

Consequently, heroin and other drugs of its class produce a profound sense of well-being, comfort, and freedom from pain when administered. Other effects of opiates are nausea, constipation, and sleepiness.

Heroin can be snorted in powder form, smoked from aluminum foil (called "chasing the dragon"), and, of course, injected intravenously. Codeine, Vicodin, Percodan, and Darvon occur in pill form and are usually medically prescribed.

Opiate overdose results in profound sleepiness, vomiting, suppression of the normal protective cough reflexes, respiratory suppression, respiratory arrest, and death. Heroin is rapidly, extremely, physiologically addictive, and the withdrawal syndrome lasts two to three days and includes sweating, tremor, nausea, severe body pain, and depression. There is a currently new and controversial treatment for opiate addiction called Rapid Detox. In this approach, the individual is chemically paralyzed (fully anesthetized), intubated, and placed on a ventilator (breathing machine). While the individual is completely unconscious and paralyzed, the body is flooded with intravenous Narcan (naloxone). Narcan is a chemical (usually used in emergency rooms in the treatment of acute opiate overdose) that binds extremely tightly to the body's opiate receptors and displaces all of the opiate drug molecules from the receptors. While naloxone is present in the body, no opiate molecule can bind to any available opiate receptors, and the "high" is completely reversed and terminated.

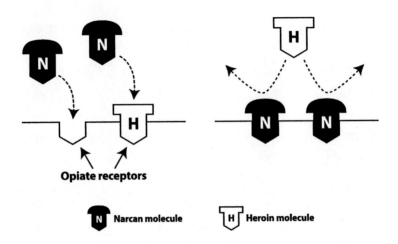

Opiate receptors

N Narcan molecule   H Heroin molecule

All that remains is to flush out all of the displaced opiates from the patient's blood stream with intravenously-administered fluids and diuretics (medicines which stimulate urination) over the next four to six hours. If the patient were awake, he/she would experience an acutely intense drug withdrawal reaction. However, since the patient is fully anesthetized and paralyzed and is being maintained on life support (ventilator breathing machine), he/she is awakened after the acute withdrawal reaction has passed with no unpleasant memory or experience of it. This procedure in some ways is a marvelous advancement. However, since the horrible experience of acute opiate withdrawal can be avoided, wealthy addicts tend to return immediately to drug use since they know that they can afford to undergo the rapid detox procedure again for another few thousand dollars whenever they feel they have "had enough."

Heroin, "the big H," is usually shot intravenously so that it enters the heart and blood stream quickly and gets you "up there" in a hurry. Heroin is *physi-ologically* addictive and creates a *psychological* dependency as well. This drug can be cleared out of the physical body in about two weeks; that is, the physiological addiction can be cured in that time. But most of these "cured" addicts will walk out of a hospital and go right out to get another fix because they have to have it psychologically. It becomes a crutch that they cannot do without.

With heroin, it's almost as if a barrier is placed between the nerves. It's not a bridging, as it is with hallucinogenics. It's more like a hardening formation. If you've ever looked at an addict who's been shooting a lot of heroin, you'll probably see that their skin appears thick. It's as though the nerve impulses have to come pounding through if they are going to be able to bridge the synapses. It's like the difference between slapping bare skin and slapping skin through a shirt. The impulses keep building up, the barrier between the nerves builds up, and the feeling response gradually thickens. This shows up in someone who has been shooting for ten or twelve years. One shot of heroin won't do this to you; neither will two or three. But much more than that, and you're probably on your way.

Marijuana

Cannabis, marijuana, pot, weed, hashish, grass, whatever you want to call it—this is the one that people say won't hurt you. Many people say it's non-addicting. It's not like other drugs; it won't harm you. Because of statements and attitudes like these, we consider it the most dangerous drug of all. True, it's not addicting physiologically, but neither is LSD or many of the "uppers." But all of these create a psychological dependency that is tremendously powerful—more powerful than physical addiction. People who have become addicted to drugs through a hospital program can usually be withdrawn from the drug, walk out of the hospital, and never miss it at all. *Psychological* dependency is a far greater problem.

Let's say that the conscious and subconscious minds are moving along within their normal patterns, and at some point you smoke a joint of marijuana. It probably won't do anything much for you; it will probably be a nothing. You might feel a little nauseated, but not much. You smoke another, and you start getting a little bit high. It's very easy, no big jolts, and you come back down again. No adverse effects, no problems (that you are aware of). You might have gotten just a little high and found it sort of pleasant, so you try it again some time. This time, you smoke a little more, go a little "higher." Maybe you start to lose your balance and your perspective, and you put it down and don't smoke anymore.

But suppose, for whatever reason, that you continue to smoke pot and you smoke it more often and smoke more of it. At first, the pattern of the subconscious mind becomes a little bit different from that of the conscious mind, but not enough to notice. It continues to split off from the conscious mind, however; the gap widens and the communication between the subconscious mind and conscious mind becomes blocked.

As you continue to smoke pot, the pattern of the subconscious mind becomes more erratic, more jagged. If the conscious mind is strong, you can continue smoking marijuana for quite a long time without the effects or changes showing too much. But the changes are taking place on the subconscious level. Eventually, it may reach the point where it will start the same reaction pattern as with other addictive drugs, but it comes on so gradually and so subtly that you may not realize that you have gotten locked into that new pattern. You're out of control; then you have to smoke not to get high, but just to maintain a feeling of normalcy. You find that if you let yourself come down, you're really a mess, so you continually smoke to stay "normal." Then, in an effort to get high or in an effort to break out of this pattern, you may go on to the hard stuff—speed, heroin, something that is injected or ingested that will give you a faster, "higher high." And then you have to inject more and more to maintain yourself at that point. You can end up supporting a very expensive habit.

So many young people who smoke pot heavily have come to me knowing that the drugs were affecting them and asking for help. They've been told that marijuana is OK, that it's not addictive and doesn't do any harm. But their experience is different. I've had people tell me that they can't think, they can't really control themselves, and they seem to flip back into feeling high when they haven't been smoking.

They're right, and it can be a big step in the right direction when a person recognizes it for themselves. Some people will keep arguing that it just can't be harmful and that they are making it up. Too many times, this is the approach people use when they talk to others, especially young people, about pot. But the person smoking dope will say, "LOOK! Take a look and see what's going on." If you do take a look at someone you know who is smoking dope, you have to say, "You're right; something has really changed you."

The terrible thing here is that the conscious mind tries to continue on, but the subconscious mind has thrown itself out of balance and just can't make it. Some of these people are trying to find God. They're trying to expand their consciousness and find out what's going on. If a person who decides to smoke grass to increase their spiritual awareness reaches that point of awareness they were seeking, and then never touches marijuana again, it can be looked at as a positive action. But 99.99 percent of the time, they don't do this. Either they're after a kick or thrills in the first place, or they lose track of their original goal of higher awareness once they start smoking, and then go the familiar route of deterioration.

Marijuana has a variety of effects on people and the timing of those effects is unpredictable. One factor that contributes to the instability of pot and other illicit drugs is that they are mixed with various things. You can't be really sure of what you're getting. This can make a big difference to whoever uses them.

A person's reaction to pot and to drugs in general depends upon many things as well as the drug itself. It depends upon the strength of your conscious and subconscious minds. It depends upon your structure and your personality traits. It depends upon your genetics, your environment, your emotional stability, and your spiritual evolvement. It depends upon whether you're going to drink or do other drugs in combination while you use. It depends upon your physical condition when you use. Anyone's response depends upon a wide variety of factors, and *all* of them need to be taken into consideration.

One person might smoke pot or use drugs on occasion and have nothing happen. Another might smoke pot or use drugs once and kill themselves. We know of one person who smoked some hash and jumped out of his window (which was on the second story), broke both his legs, crawled across to where a girl was, and killed her "because God said she had to go." The authorities thought he was psychotic until they started checking and talking to his friends, who told them that he had been smoking hash and was "higher than a kite" when they left him before the killing. There is also a case history of a girl who was driving with her boyfriend on the freeway. She told him he was going too slow and that it would be faster if she walked; she got out of the car when it was going eighty miles an hour and killed herself. These are true incidents and might happen after smoking one joint or many. You cannot tell what the reaction is going to be. Marijuana distorts your perceptions.

Marijuana also attacks and rips the etheric body just like you would rip a piece of paper. The rip often occurs in a place corresponding to the reticular formation of the brain and, also, in a place corresponding to the pituitary gland, which is the master gland of the body. When the etheric body is ripped, the life-energy forces spill out because they're not being channeled through the natural chakra openings of the body.

Then, instead of coming through the aura patterns in a beautiful flow, the life force flows out through the rips, and the aura or the etheric body becomes sticky, like honey or molasses.

If you are skilled, you can tell if someone has had any type of drugs in their body because, as you run your hand through their aura, it feels sticky and your hand sort of drags, as if you were moving through oatmeal. The good news is that the rips can be sealed so that the energy can again flow in the natural way, though it takes someone who is trained and skilled to repair this type of damage.[1] And you must be ready to give up smoking dope, or you will simply re-create the problem. There is a raging debate over the legitimate medical use of marijuana prescribed for the treatment of glaucoma (to reduce the pressure with the eyes), cancer, and HIV (to stimulate appetite and reduce pain). This controversy is as yet unsettled.

As we said at the beginning of this chapter, people often smoke marijuana or hash thinking it has no negative effects and that it is not addictive, making it one of the more dangerous drugs.

---

[1] The Movement of Spiritual Inner Awareness (MSIA) offers aura balances, which can help repair the rips in the etheric body and aura caused by drug abuse. For more information, call the MSIA office: (323) 737-4055 or go to www.msia.org

Cocaine

Cocaine was initially chewed as a leaf by South American Indians for its stimulant effect. Cocaine was also used as a local anesthetic before stronger, less expensive and less psychoactive anesthetics were developed. Cocaine has two major effects brought on by enhancing the actions of two major neurotransmitters (chemicals responsible for transmission of nerve impulses in the body).

1. *Cocaine's first major effect:* Cocaine blocks the reuptake of norepinephrine from the synapses

between neurons leading to both central and peripheral nervous system excitement.

a. Arriving from neuron I, a nerve impulse reaches the synapse and norepinephrine is released across the synaptic space causing transmission of the impulse to the next neuron (neuron II).

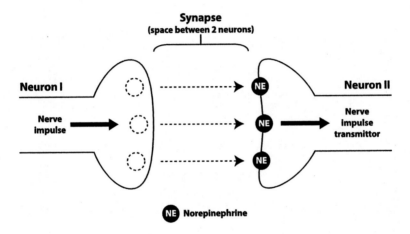

b. Following this transmission, norepinephrine is normally removed from the synapse (called norepinephrine reuptake) and returned to neuron I, terminating continued stimulation of neuron II.

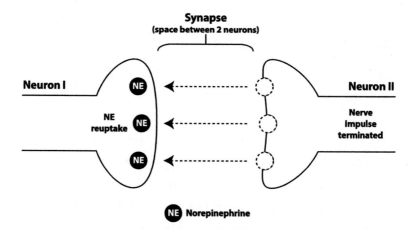

Synapse
(space between 2 neurons)

Neuron I

NE

NE reuptake

NE

NE

Neuron II

Nerve impulse terminated

NE Norepinephrine

c. Cocaine blocks the removal (reuptake) of norepinephrine from neuron II, thus causing continued sustained stimulation across the synapse. This is the cocaine "high."

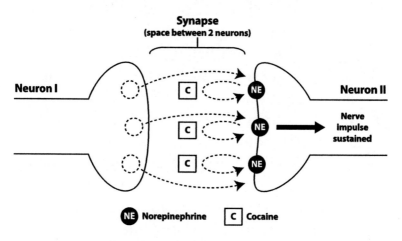

Synapse
(space between 2 neurons)

Neuron I

C

C

C

NE

NE

NE

Neuron II

Nerve impulse sustained

NE Norepinephrine   C Cocaine

Another name for norepinephrine is noradrenaline, and the effects of increased adrenaline levels should be familiar to you as the way the body feels during nervousness, anxiousness, anger, or fright.

In addition to the above-illustrated central and peripheral nervous system stimulation, cocaine has a second major effect.

2. *Cocaine's second major effect:* Cocaine causes the release of dopamine directly. Dopamine is a neurotransmitter within the central nervous system that stimulates the brain's pleasure centers. By these two mechanisms, cocaine induces both excitement and euphoria. Some men experience intense stimulation with complete impotence. It can be sexually stimulating, either with or without associated impotence.

   Cocaine can be snorted, injected, or, most notoriously, smoked. When converted to its freebase form—which is accomplished by boiling powdered cocaine with baking soda, resulting in a solid that is easily vaporized —cocaine can be smoked as freebase or crack. When smoked in this way, the rush can be as stimulating and euphoric as an intravenous injection because the lungs take up the chemicals so rapidly and easily. So intense is the crack or freebase high that many individuals experience an immediate, consuming addiction after the very first exposure ("hit").

   Powdered cocaine tends to be relatively expensive, while crack is much cheaper and easier to purchase; it is also much more intensely addictive. The rush from freebasing lasts for only three to four minutes. As with most addictive substances, the individual quickly needs greater and greater amounts to reach the level of the previous hit. As previously described, the individual's focus of activity eventually shifts (gradually or quickly) from normal life patterns to activities centered only around obtaining and using the drug.

There is a unique and characteristic paranoia associated with continued cocaine use, as well as long-term amphetamine use called "tweeking" that involves closing windows and blinds, locking doors, turning off lights, obsession with intruders, and feelings of being watched. The use of cocaine quickly passes from the initial euphoric stage and moves into the paranoid state.

Fortunately, withdrawal from cocaine is largely psychological and minimally physiological, unlike the opiate withdrawal with its short-term tremors, nausea, convulsions, and pain, or benzodiazepine withdrawal with its long-term aches, body and joint pains, tremors, and risk of seizures. Cocaine withdrawal usually involves agitation, feelings of despair, depression, and irritability, etc. However, the psychological addiction can be extremely powerful.

7

Specialty Drugs

PCP: Phencyclidine (angel dust), sherm, embalming fluid, or rocket fuel. PCP was initially developed as an anesthetic, but because of its extreme side effects, including delirium, confusion, and hallucinations, it is now only used as a tranquilizer for animals. It is often listed in its own class of drugs because of its unique effects: a combination of suppression, stimulation, and hallucination. There is a classic case in urban emergency rooms of the naked, sweating, psychotic PCP user who has displayed extremely violent aggression, broken through handcuffs with his bare hands, and who is so disinhibited that four or five policeman were required to subdue the person. The combination of effects produced by PCP includes complete disorientation, violent aggression, auditory and visual hallucinations, loss of perception of pain, extreme perspiration, etc. PCP occurs as a powder or liquid which is applied to marijuana (super weed), mint leaves, or tobacco (sherm), and rolled into joints and smoked, or smoked in a pipe.

GHB: Blue nitro, liquid X, midnight blue, somax somatopro. GHB was initially used at low doses as an alternative to steroids for body builders because it was thought to increase the secretion of growth hormone by the brain's pituitary gland. It is usually a liquid but may be a powder that can be mixed into an alcoholic drink. Eventually GHB was noticed to cause profound depression of consciousness, euphoria, and intoxication, leading to its more widespread use, especially among youth attending rave parties, and in sexual situations. Because of its reliable effect of depression of consciousness with memory loss, GHB is often used as a date rape drug. At low doses, GHB causes euphoria and release of inhibitions. However, at only slightly higher doses, it can produce profound coma, seizures, and death. This drug is especially dangerous because tiny increases in dosage may cause dramatic increases in effects in as little as 15 minutes and accidental overdoses are extremely likely.

Ketamine: Vitamin K, special K. This drug is actually an anesthetic that was commonly used in the field during the Vietnam war. It is also a cat tranquilizer used legitimately by veterinarians in an intravenous injectable liquid form. Illicit ketamine is a powder which is inhaled or swallowed in pill form. Ketamine is often described as a less potent version of PCP, another more powerful animal tranquilizer. Ketamine use is popular at rave parties along with MDA (speed) and GHB. Ketamine produces a disassociative anesthetic state in which the user experiences amnesia (memory loss) and analgesia (loss of sensation to pain). The drug may produce dream-like states and hallucinations. Flashbacks can occur with ketamine. Ketamine overdose results in slurred speech, dizziness, and confusion, which may progress to respiratory arrest, cardiac arrest, and death. The profoundly depressed state of consciousness and near-death experience produced just by 0.5 grams of ketamine is called the K hole. Long-term use produces short-term memory loss, impaired vision, and reduced attention span.

Nitrous Oxide: Laughing gas. This is a weak anesthetic gas most often used in dentistry. Nitrous oxide is inhaled usually from a small balloon that has been filled from a small high-pressure canister. These canisters (whippets) are normally intended for producing whipped cream. They are also available in head shops (smoke shops), specifically for elicit use. These are called crackers. For use at parties, large pressurized tanks of nitrous oxide are even available. Following a single deep inhalation, the intoxicating effects last one or two minutes and include a tingling sensation, spinning, disorientation, fixated vision, pulsating auditory and/or visual hallucinations, and an increased pain threshold. Nitrous oxide use can lead to complete loss of motor control and the user may fall to the floor and experience bodily harm. People have even died by suffocation from breathing pure nitrous oxide with no oxygen mixed in. Nausea and vomiting may occur, especially if the user has recently eaten. Addiction is a real possibility and addicts may experience mood and personality changes. Bone marrow and nervous system damage may occur with prolonged use and may require B-12 injections over several days to help overcome the problem.

Glue Sniffing: Glue sniffing is a general term that refers to inhaling the fumes of model airplane glue, gasoline, paint thinner, lighter fluid, or even white-out correction fluid. These toxic liquids are usually applied to a cloth, and the cloth is then held over the nose and mouth and vigorously inhaled. This form of drug abuse is more popular among young users, age 9 to 15 years old. The active ingredients include alcohol, chloroform, and toluene (especially toxic to the kidneys). Initial symptoms include muscular incoordination, slurred speech, blurred vision, mild hallucinations, nausea, depression, and ringing in the ears lasting from 30-45 minutes. Heavy intoxication may lead to stupor or unconsciousness. These chemicals are true poisons. Their continued use will inevitably lead to brain damage, kidney damage, liver damage, bone marrow toxicity, and loss of vision. Physical dependence does not occur, but psychological dependence on the euphoric effects may develop over time. The practice of glue sniffing is extremely poisonous and is rapidly, seriously damaging to various organs of the body.

Amyl Nitrate: poppers, rush, climax. Amyl nitrate was originally used as a short-term treatment for chest pain (angina). It has been replaced by nitroglycerine. Amyl nitrate dilates the blood vessels causing a drop in blood pressure and an increase in heart rate. It is the sudden dilation of blood vessels in the brain that gives the euphoric effect. Amyl nitrate is a liquid whose vapors are typically inhaled from a small bottle for desired effect, usually during sexual activity and most often when the user is approaching orgasm. This practice is more popular among the gay community for some reason. Short-term adverse reactions include skin and mucus membrane irritation, nausea, headache, loss of consciousness, cardiac arrhythmias, and possibly sudden death. Chronic use may lead to permanent neurological damage, as well as medically documented suppression of the body's immune system, allowing increased viral reproduction in HIV positive persons.

Intravenous Drug Abuse: Special Dangers

There are specific risks associated with the intravenous injection of any of the various types of injectable drugs: heroin, speed, cocaine, Demerol, etc.

1. HIV: sharing needles with other persons can lead to the accidental transfer of tiny amounts of contaminated blood from one person to another,

transmitting HIV and AIDS viruses requiring life-long treatment.

2. Hepatitis B and C: Sharing needles can lead to the accidental transfer of viruses that infect the liver, causing hepatitis B and C, which may result in liver damage, death, or result in a lifelong carrier state and an increased risk of liver cancer.

3. Endocarditis: Use of needles without adequate skin cleansing can cause accidental injection of bacteria into the blood stream that preferentially attack the heart valves and the lining of the heart, causing endocarditis, requiring prolonged hospitalization and IV antibiotics for four to six weeks.

4. Cellulitis: Use of needles without adequate skin cleansing can also cause infections of the soft tissues of the arms, legs, or other injection sites called cellulitis, requiring prolonged antibiotic therapy in or out of the hospital.

5. Local abscesses and scarring: Use of needles without adequate skin cleansing often results in local pockets of pus (abscesses) which must be opened, drained and treated with antibiotics, leaving multiple scars. These can be quite painful.

6. Venous sclerosis: (Hardening) Repeated injections into the same vein causes hardening and stricture, rendering the vein useless. Long-term addicts

may use up their available injection sites (arms, legs, hands, feet, and even the neck), making intravenous access difficult when true medical emergencies arise. These scarred veins are called "tracks."

Because of these serious, additional risks associated with shooting up, intravenous drug users would be well advised to thoroughly flush their needles with bleach before and after each use, and to never share their needles with another person.

Dual Diagnosis Persons

Persons who suffer from both drug or alcohol abuse *and* other psychological disorders (such as obsessive compulsive disorder, bi-polar disorder, depression, psychosis, etc.) fall into a category called Dual Diagnosis. These persons require definitive psychiatric care (often including psychiatric medications, hospitalizations, and psychotherapy) for their psychological disorder, as well as intensive rehabilitation for substance abuse. In these types of patients, neither underlying problem can be easily corrected without simultaneous treatment of both disorders. This can be an especially challenging situation from which to recover.

Drug/Alcohol Abuse During Pregnancy

Chronic alcohol consumption during pregnancy can lead to a special set of characteristic birth defects called fetal alcohol syndrome, which includes low birth weight, mental retardation, and structural defects of the face and heart.

Besides the definitive birth defects that can be caused by alcohol consumption during pregnancy, abuse of opiates and cocaine (in particular), as well as speed and some other drugs, frequently leads to the birth of "addicted babies."

Drug abuse during pregnancy causes the fetus to develop in a biochemical environment where the drug of choice is frequently present in its bloodstream. Upon delivery from the mother, the baby's blood supply of addicting drugs is cut off and the infant goes into physiological withdrawal including respiratory distress, tremor, poor feeding, failure to grow, diarrhea/vomiting, and often, death.

Alcohol

Through alcohol abuse, people can destroy the natural rhythms of their consciousness in the same ways as with drugs, though in a slightly different process. Unlike amphetamines or cocaine, which alter consciousness by enhancing the transmission, release, and activities of neurotransmitters across the synapses, alcohol *sensitizes* the neurons of the body to the inhibiting effects of certain specialized neurotransmitters, which slow down and eventually shut down the transmission of nerve impulses between the nerves. Also, alcohol directly increases the release of endorphins (which bind to and stimulate opiate receptors) and dopamine (a pleasure inducing neurotransmitter) in the central nervous system.

Since the higher brain centers (which are responsible for application of the learned controls over instinctive behaviors, decision making, etc.) are among the most sensitive, it is the normal behavioral inhibitions and the ability to make normally appropriate decisions that are generally first affected by alcohol intoxication. Continued use of alcohol leads to loss of muscular coordination and eventually blackout.

Alcohol stimulates the blood and dilates the blood vessels. Then, as it reaches the capillaries, it's like pouring straight alcohol into your blood, causing the capillaries to constrict. That constriction shuts down the nerve energy and the oxygen flow into the front part of the brain, leaving only the back part of the brain, the reactive part, functioning. So you think you're doing really well, but there's very little thinking ability left; at this point, you're slurring your speech a little bit, too.

The blood vessels that supply the brain come up through the carotid artery. The farthest extension of this goes into the areas that control the most highly developed areas of sensitivity and muscle coordination. Alcohol inhibits synaptic impulse transmission, and the brain starts shutting itself down from front to back. The first part to become deadened will usually be the area that controls the eyes, followed by the speech centers, and then the area that controls the extremities (the hands and feet). As the constriction continues, it starts to deaden the bowel area, the kidneys, and other central body functions. It shuts off the control and disables these functions one by one.

Alcohol shuts down the *thinking* area, as do marijuana, LSD, and others, and then the *reactive* area goes out of control. As the reactive part of the brain becomes dominant, the person sometimes becomes belligerent and they may want to get into a fight and "really show you." You can't reason with them. They may hit you, and you say, "You crazy nut, I'm your friend," and they say, "I don't care, I'll hit you again," because they're not thinking.

Then they usually start feeling pretty sexy because the thinking mind and inhibitions are down, including the part that would ordinarily say, "Watch it, friend, there's danger around here." They couldn't care less. If they keep drinking, the sexual area shuts down. By then, all direction is gone. This might only take five or six drinks of a two-ounce glass of hard liquor during an hour-and-a-half to two-hour period. Then the medulla oblongata, in the lower portion of the brainstem, shuts down from the neck down. At this point, they is no more than a sequence of spinal reactions. By then they can't even walk. The heart is going and the respiration is going; everything else is "dead." There is very little circulation going on in the brain.

If a person drinks excessively over an extended period of time, the pituitary gland and the thalamus, which ordinarily are highly protected, may be affected. Then the organs start shutting down, one after the other. The first organ hit will usually be the liver. Liver damage, including fatty infiltration, alcoholic hepatitis, enlargement, scarring, and eventual cirrhosis, along with alcoholic gastritis (irritation and scarring) and gastric bleeding of the lining of the stomach are classic consequences of chronic alcohol abuse, as well as cardiac enlargement and brain damage. When this starts, the person has just about had it. This can be the big awakener, when the person goes to a doctor who may say it's cirrhosis. By then there may already be permanent damage.

Many end-stage alcoholics eventually require liver transplants. It raises an interesting ethical question as to whether it is really appropriate to "waste" a donated liver on an alcoholic (who will probably eventually destroy the donated organ as well) versus giving these precious organs to nonaddicted persons.

Expression of alcoholism is complex, including functional alcoholics who may drink almost daily but never to the point of impairment of their job performance. These persons may last for years until they are confronted by the medical consequences of their addiction (liver damage, gastric bleeding, etc.). Periodic alcoholics or binge drinkers may drink to excess only on occasions varying from weekends only, to once a month, to once every six months only, etc. Blackout drinkers have no control over their alcohol intake and invariably drink into a complete blackout where they do not remember where they have been or what they have done. Daily alcoholics are the classic alcoholics who drink every day and smell of alcohol at work in the morning or anytime.

Withdrawal from chronic alcohol abuse can also be dangerous. Delirium tremens refers to psychosis and seizures associated with sudden withdrawal from chronic alcohol abuse. These seizures can be violent and life-threatening. One of the truly acceptable medical uses of short-term benzodiazepines (Valium, Ativan) is to prevent the characteristic seizures associated with the first two weeks of therapy for the alcoholic who is trying to quit.

Remember from the explanation in the introduction of this book that, in addition to possessing various dispositions toward alcoholism, including peer pressure, personality traits, stress, and karmic path, alcoholics are genetically and biochemically different from normal people. Alcoholics metabolize alcohol along completely different chemical side reactions than most people do, producing, among other things, TIQQs which give them an opiate-like euphoric sensation that is not experienced by an average person consuming alcohol.

Rehabilitation for alcoholism is in some ways much more difficult than rehabilitation from illicit street drugs, since the alcoholic has to face advertisements and confront socially acceptable use of his drug of choice (alcohol) on an almost daily basis. Unlike the crack addict, for example, who will never encounter crack magazine or TV ads, see rows of crack for sale at his grocery store while he is shopping, or casually be offered crack while dining out, alcoholics are surrounded by a culture that promotes alcohol use as a normal part of everyday life.

The difference between alcohol and drugs to the human consciousness is about the same as the difference between a 38 caliber pistol and a 45 caliber pistol. They can both kill you.

As with other drugs, alcohol also affects the aura, or electromagnetic energy field around your body. These effects can last for a very long time, but they can be cleared with techniques such as aura balancing, which is described at the end of this book. We have seen people come in for an aura balance who may have drunk beer or wine with their friends many years ago and who still carry the sticky effects in their aura. If you are ready to move on to the greater adventures of Spirit, we recommend having the aura balances to clear you from the effects of alcohol and other drugs.

Using alcohol is a form of giving up your responsibility for your own consciousness. One of the lesser-known side effects is that, as soon as you feel that "letting go," or loosening up of your body and mind, you are also opening yourself up to psychic influences that you may not enjoy. Getting drunk is a way of saying, "I don't want to be responsible right now for my thoughts or actions. I'm taking a break." While you're on "vacation," you've left your "home" open to what we call disincarnate entities. They can legally move in and begin to influence you according to *their* wants and desires rather than your own. The reason these beings are staying close to earth looking for a body to influence is usually because they are deeply attached to something on this earth: alcohol, sex, or other strong desires. Once you are under the influence of a disincarnate entity, you may find yourself moving into patterns that weren't previously part of your normal functioning. It's well known that one way to tell if people are doing drugs or drinking alcohol heavily is that their personalities and interests seem to change. Often this is because of the influence of entities that have attached themselves to these people and are exerting their influence.

Both red and white wine are very popular social drinks. An entire culture and tradition have built up around them, and many people enjoy a glass or two fairly often. Red wine in particular seems to have a great many entities closely involved with it, just waiting to move in on the people drinking it.

Clearing these negative influences can be done. It often takes a combination of spiritual assistance, and most of all, your being ready to let them go. You do this by building your personal inner strength through making better choices for your self, through spiritual practices, and by no longer doing the things, like drinking or drugs, that allow negative influences into your consciousness.

This information is not meant to create fear; it is for your education. You decide for yourself what works *for* you. As always, check things out for yourself. Ask yourself good questions, then listen and observe closely to get your answers. Why do you drink? What are the drawbacks? How are your relationships, your work, your interests affected? Are there better ways to get what you really want without harming yourself or others? Track your experiences, and take a good look at what's going on with you. That way, you are learning and growing.

Making Wise Choices

This is a planet of the sword. A sword has two sharp edges: one is positive for hewing something beautiful, and the other is negative for destroying. You have to be open and accept, which also means that you have to *select* the things you participate in. If you resist, you get stuck. Jesus said, "Resist not evil." When you resist, negativity has something to latch onto. When you accept and let things flow, negativity will go right past you.

This process works in several ways around drugs. Your choices about drugs include whom you choose to spend your time with. If you spend a lot of time around people who indulge in drugs, you run the danger of picking up these patterns in your aura even if you are not taking drugs yourself. As these patterns permeate your auric field, they begin to influence you; you can fall into the patterns of drug usage and begin to take drugs. If you don't wish to involve yourself with drugs, it's best to stay away from areas and people where drugs are being used.

We have been explaining the effects of drugs on the body and various levels of consciousness. Now let's talk about another level of consciousness. There is a greater level, a source from which all people come. We call this source God or Spirit. Every human being is connected to that source and is a part of it. The part of us that is connected to Spirit, we call the Soul; every person has one. We call the energy that flows from God, from the source, Light.

In the Soul and the higher realms of Spirit, this Light is invisible. But it also flows through every level of our consciousness in this world. It is what touches us when we read or hear truth (the mind), when we feel happy, joyful, and uplifted (the emotions), and when we are energized through the good things that we do (the body). Ultimately, our high self (see page 9) knows what is best for us and nudges us toward the highest, best choices. Our basic self, although it can easily get stuck in habits, is often most happy when we are living in a way that keeps us healthy and well, since its job is to take care of the body. We have a lot going for us.

This world is a school, designed to make us strong and help us learn to make wise choices. We are tested all the time. What is the prize? A surprising one, as it may not look like much in the world, but there is nothing greater: awareness of ourselves as a Soul having experiences in this world, learning, growing, and ultimately, returning to our home in Spirit.

There was a young man who had great potential. He was being taught about the Light and the action of the Light, and he could have moved into an expression of Light consciousness. But he also went to a lot of pot parties with his friends. He was told about the drug action and he said, "I go into the group, and I send them the Light and love them all, so everything is okay."

It was explained to him how he could get suckered right into the drug scene because it was a potential karmic path for him. He was at a choice point of either accepting it and going that way or stepping away from it. He had the knowledge and the ability to choose another path. He said that he did not want to leave his friends, so the recommendation was: "Get new friends."

Well, he was a free Soul. No one controlled his life. He's so hooked on narcotics now that his mind is shot. You'll be talking to him about one thing and he'll go off on a tangent. You try to get him back to the subject and he sort of comes back and then takes off again. His mind is following what to him is a logical pattern, but he doesn't know that his mouth isn't matching it. And he thinks *you're* weird because you're not keeping up with him. This is one of those cases where it's his right to destroy himself as he chooses. And it's his responsibility to go through every bit of the action. The problem is that there is no foundation for spiritual illumination through the illusions involved with drugs.

There's an old saying that can be applied to the use of drugs: "Once a philosopher, twice an addict." You could try drugs once, but it's not necessary to try everything. If you saw someone put his hand on a hot stove and get burned, you wouldn't do it. You'd believe that it would burn you, too. Some people don't believe it, and they'll have to touch the stove themselves and say, "Oh, that's hot." After four or five dozen have done that, others might say, "You know, there might be something about this that will burn." Some people are sharp enough to watch other people's experiences and learn from them. We call it vicarious functioning. This is when we get to be students in a big way.

If you judge those who are involved with drugs, you lock some of your energy up in that judgment and you are not free to move into your own full expression. We can't judge those who are involved with drugs, but we can help them get beyond these drug-induced experiences.

10

Recovery Programs

Approaches to Recovery Programs

Statistically, much less than half of addicts ever retain long-term sobriety. Various services available to addicts/alcoholics range from AA programs to outpatient rehabilitation programs to inpatient rehabilitation programs to sober living homes to rehabilitation on one's own.

AA Program

The AA program has several forms—AA for alcoholics, CA for cocaine addicts, NA for narcotics addicts, SA for sex addicts, and OA for overeating addicts. The underlying basis for all of these addictions is approximately the same. The AA program is statistically the most reliably successful rehabilitation program. The AA approach involves personal admission and acceptance of powerlessness over drugs and alcohol, regular attendance at AA meetings where one hears the inspirational stories of successfully recovering addicts, acceptance of a higher power capable of pulling the addict out of the addiction, willingness to maintain a close personal, nonsexual relationship with a sponsor (a successfully recovering addict with at least two years continuous sobriety with whom you connect), willingness to follow that sponsor's direction, and the systematic and regular completion of 12 steps in which the addict undergoes various processes. For example, the recovering addict may list all those he has wronged, making personal amends where possible, and confront underlying personal issues which are often the basis of addiction (childhood abuse, self-hatred, low self-esteem, etc.). AA is easily accessible by simply calling 411 information in your town; regular meetings are widespread throughout the country, especially in urban centers. It is important, especially in the early phases of recovery, to realize that you are not alone and to substitute the previous network of practicing addicts and enablers with a new set of contacts and support network of recovering people. AA has two widely accepted textbooks on recovery, *The Big Book of AA* and *The 12 Steps of Recovery*.

Outpatient Rehabilitation

Most inpatient rehabilitation programs offer regular sessions which are open to nonresident addicts from the outside. These are excellent sessions to attend because they allow exposure to the more intense processes and exercises which are utilized by inpatient facilities, as well as exposure to trained health care professionals who specialize in addiction (they often make presentations) without actually having to incur the expense and inconvenience of inpatient residential treatment.

Inpatient Rehabilitation

For those who can afford it, and those for whom it is court mandated, inpatient rehabilitation offers the individual immediate structure and complete immersion into a lifestyle centered around recovery 24 hours a day without outside distractions. These programs usually last one to three months initially. However, for repeat offenders who are court-referred or for people with especially difficult addictions, inpatient treatment may last as long as ten months to one year.

The total number of inpatients in a facility is usually around 30 or so. A typical day in inpatient rehab involves awakening around 7:00 a.m., personal hygiene and making the bed, a morning walk followed by breakfast around 9:00 a.m., in-house meetings, late morning educational presentations (including videos or lectures from staff professionals), lunch, early afternoon AA meeting or regular exercise activity or open meeting available to addicts from the outside, late afternoon study periods involving reading recovery-related materials (*Big Book* or *AA 12-Step Book*), counseling sessions, and completion of assignments. Dinner and supervised attendance at outside AA meetings generally occur in the evening, followed by a final in-house discussion group session prior to lights out around 11:00 p.m. Weekends usually involve chores and other cleaning and facility maintenance-oriented tasks assigned to each participant. Family visits may also occur. Random urine testing is usually enforced in inpatient rehabilitation centers to ensure abstinence.

Sober Living Facilities

Following completion of an inpatient rehab program, the participant is often referred to a sober living facility. These are group homes with usually around 10-15 people in which recovering persons have a semi-supervised lifestyle providing room and board, while they go out during the day to seek or perform work. There is a curfew usually around 6:30 p.m. or so and the participant must be back inside for dinner and then attend an in-house evening AA meeting. Residence in a sober living home may last anywhere from months to one-two years.

Physical Exercise

Regular rigorous physical exercise is scientifically proven to aid in recovery from addiction. The cardiovascular effects increase the cleansing of the body of toxins and accumulated drug metabolic by-products.

Exercise offers a structured, rewarding alternative activity to drug behavior and directly produces a natural, endorphin-mediated sense of well-being.

It is important to intervene as early as possible in the course of an individual's addiction. The difficulty lies in determining who is addicted and who is not. There is no simple test. Exactly the same simple recreational marijuana use may not be an addictive behavior for some individuals, but it may lead to an all-consuming addiction in others. Exactly the same amount of alcohol per week in one person may be fine, yet a sign of a profound addiction in another.

Simple recreational use of the more powerful drugs without progression to addiction is rare (although it does exist), and this is one reason the use of more powerful drugs is either strictly controlled or outlawed outright. A good test recommended in recovery circles is that the person voluntarily discontinues use of his or her drug of choice for one month or so, frequently checking for personality changes, stress, anxiety, irritability, and alterations of sleep patterns. The presence of any of these symptoms often indicates addiction, either fully developed or in progress.

Recognition and admission of addiction in one's self is the most difficult step for the recovering addict. The progression of addiction is devious and hypnotizing. The addict/alcoholic is classically in complete denial of his/her condition.

Most addicts are fully into an extensive addiction pattern before they even consider that their behavior is abnormal. Friends, loved ones, family members, and co-workers—if not the police—are usually the first signals to gain the addict's attention. Early, loving intervention is important to prevent progression of the disease of addiction and to minimize the devastating wreckage it can cause to the person's life, health, career, and personal development.

Information and education regarding addiction are crucial. It is only relatively recently that drug addiction has been approached and scientifically studied, without prejudice, as a disease process rather than a character flaw or moral failing. Indeed, the majority of the medical community is still very much in the dark regarding recent developments in the understanding of the biochemical and genetic components of addiction.

One of the purposes of this book is to provide you with exposure to these developments and to provide you with useful information to protect and assist you in helping yourself or others who may have stepped into a pattern of addiction. More detailed information is available on the Internet and in medical textbooks or may be obtained by calling any hospital-based recovery facility listed in the yellow pages.

When looking at the options available, it may be useful to consider recovery from addiction as a life-long process that requires a sustained focus by the "recoveree." The disease is not necessarily cured, as in bronchitis or an infection. It is more akin to a chronic illness that must be dealt with every day, much like high blood pressure or diabetes.

The recovering person would be well served by consistently applying him/herself toward positive activities, positive relationships, and a spiritual focus. Many recovering persons view their sobriety as a gift of grace, a reprieve granted by God. Sobriety must be nurtured, exercised, and actively pursued on a daily basis.

11

Spiritual Exercises: An Alternative To Drugs

The Light

Many people find that spiritual practices bring them what they are seeking and fulfill the desire to "get high," to experience something greater, higher, more loving, more expansive than what everyday life seems to offer. Through the Spirit, you travel inner worlds in a greater and more complete way than drugs offer, under control and protection. You are working to expand your mind and consciousness. You know where you are going, how to get there in a predictable way, and how to return any time you want. Spiritual practices are an upward path and bring continually greater results.

When you work to expand your consciousness through the Holy Spirit, the Spirit comes into the nerve area, strengthening the sheath on the nerves so that you can contain more "high voltage." Your nervous system will be able to contain more power. The Holy Spirit enters into a receptor, perhaps the mind or perhaps the Soul chakra, which is located in the crown of the head. Spirit enters in, flooding you with love, and the nerve area is filled with a different hormonal process. You are then in a state of fluidity; you are lifted and feel fantastic. The warmth that comes through you can be so tremendous that you'll say, "This is better." You are "tripping," in a sense of the word, but strictly under self-control.

When you ask for the Light to leave you, it lifts back up again, leaving an imprint so that the next time you ask for the Spirit to come, it comes through your body more easily. The channel is already there. As you become stronger and stronger, you can contain greater energies of the Light. The Light will come in and surround you; if you're out of balance, it will enter into specific areas to bring balance.

One day when the paramagnetic force fields of the body are all in line, the Light goes through the body and then you *are* the Light. It might take a while, but when the Light has gone through you, there can be no separation.

As you continue to expand your channel, allowing the Light to come through you, it flows through all your nerve endings, your eyes, your mouth, your fingertips, and your blood. All the time it's flowing, you're gaining strength physically, morally, mentally, and spiritually.

This happens to each one of you as you bring yourself into balance in every area of your life. Through the action of the Holy Spirit, you can bridge the nerve synapses and receive your spiritual birth, your spiritual knowing. You can take off and get high spiritually. When you return to your everyday awareness, the Spirit is present, screening away the things you don't need, automatically deflecting the things that are not for you. By bringing in the Holy Spirit, you can increase your body functions so that you can arc across the nerves and enjoy these things in the very protected environment of the Spirit.

Spiritual Exercises

People meditate for many reasons, including to calm the emotions, quiet the mind, release stress, and experience a greater sense of well-being. Most techniques that are used are passive, where you attempt to keep your body and mind still. That is nearly impossible to do. We are giving you another aspect of meditation, which changes it from a passive technique of *emptying* your mind, to an active process of *directing* your consciousness. That's why we call these *spiritual* exercises. You will be giving your mind something to do, and the focus is spiritual.

When you do spiritual exercises, you are beginning to deal with the Soul, another level of consciousness beyond the mind, body, emotions, and unconscious. We define the Soul as a dynamic, creative unit of energy, alive in the truest sense of the word. It is a part of every person. It never dies, always exists, always is. One aspect of doing spiritual exercises is becoming aware that you are a Soul, you are divine, and that as a Soul you are an extension of God. The Soul is a Divine spark, your ever-present connection to God. The other levels of consciousness—your body, mind, emotions, unconscious, etc.—are not your true essence. They are vehicles for experiencing and learning.

Because the Soul is alive and dynamic, you must get moving and active in order to know it. The exercises we are giving you are techniques of chanting sacred names of God. In addition to giving your mind something to do, this connects you to an uplifting energy. Some spiritual exercises work with one specific part of your consciousness; all spiritual exercises lift you into higher, more subtle and refined states of awareness. At first, you may become more aware of (and better acquainted with) the levels of your consciousness that are part of your existence in this world: your mind, emotions, and imagination. Spiritual exercises can also break through the illusions of this world and move you into awareness of the higher levels of Soul and Spirit.

It is important to combine whatever technique of spiritual exercise you are doing with the positive power and protection of the Light. The energies that are present during spiritual exercises are subtle, but powerful. If you want success, it is essential that you ask for the power of the Light to work with you *for the highest good* during your meditation. Begin each meditation with a simple prayer, asking that the Light surround you, protect you, and fill you; that any negativity that is released be cleared and dispersed into the Light, and that all that takes place during this meditation be for the highest good. Asking this in the purity and sincerity of your own heart is your insurance that your meditation will be for your upliftment and spiritual growth.

To begin any session of spiritual exercises, choose a time and place where you won't be interrupted. If you're thirsty, drink some water. If you're hungry, get a little something to eat. Have a blanket available if you need one. Wear clothes that are comfortable and don't make you fidget. In other words, take care of possible distractions so you can relax and focus.

Take a few minutes to stretch and breathe deeply. This can help release tension from your body, mind, and emotions. Sit comfortably—but not so that you fall asleep. Close your eyes and let your body relax. Tell yourself that noises or other distractions will simply help you relax more deeply and lift higher in your consciousness.

Start by calling in the Light, as described earlier. Then you begin to chant, either silently or out loud. Choose one of the tones, or names of God, described below.

When you are done, you will want to get grounded so you're not "spacey." There are a couple good ways to do this. You can drink some water and stretch a little. You'll usually take a deep breath when you stretch, which also helps.

Another technique is to say, silently or out loud, the sound "E," as in "see." Starting with your voice pitch very low, say a long, sustained "eeeeeeeeeeee," taking the pitch from the lowest up as high as you can, and then back down low again. As you do this, imagine the sound starting at your feet, moving up through your body to a point about a foot above your head at the highest tone, then back to your feet as you go back down to the low tone. You can do this standing up. Gently reach for your toes as you start saying the "eeeee" in the low tone, then gradually reach up above your head at the high tone and back down to your toes at the low tone. It only takes a couple of seconds. Repeat it a few times, and you may be surprised at how back together you feel, balanced, centered, and ready to move on.

The Sacred Tones

The energy of the spoken word is described in the Bible as the power behind creation: God spoke the word, and there was Light. There are words, which we call tones, that are names of God and which connect back to the source. These tones are extremely powerful, yet can be subtle.

Chanting a name of God, either silently or out loud, invokes a spiritual essence and can raise the frequency

of the physical body and bring you a sense of upliftment. We introduce two sacred tones below, describ-
ing the energy they carry and ways to chant them.
There are many tones, words, mantras, or names of
God, which carry different energies with them. Some
are from lower levels. The tones we give here are
from the pure realms of the Soul and above. As you
chant them, you bring into yourself the essence of
purity, which begins replacing negativity within you.
Changes will occur within your consciousness. If you
are sincere in having Spirit as a reality in your life,
try chanting fifteen to thirty minutes a day. Regular
practice can bring about noticeable change.

HU

The "HU" reflects an ancient name of God. It invokes
the purity of that perfect God. It may be chanted in
several ways. One way is to separate it into its letters
"H" and "U," chanting a long "H..." and then shifting
to "U..." If you are chanting out loud, take in a deep
breath and, as you breath out, chant "H..." "U..." If
you are chanting silently, you might intone the "H..."
as you breathe in and the "U..." as you breathe out.
Another way to do this is to pronounce the "HU" as
one syllable (pronounced "hugh") and chant it as you
breathe out.

After you call in the Light for the highest good, a
very effective approach is to do some deep breathing before you begin to chant. Breathe in and out
five times, feeling your body fill up with the Light
energy on each breath, bringing yourself into calm,

into your center as you breathe. After five breaths, begin the chant by breathing in and chanting "HU" as you exhale. Do this for five breaths. Then repeat the process: five breaths without the chant, and five with the chant. Repeat the process one more time, so that you chant the "HU" a total of fifteen times. This will build up a lot of energy. We suggest you wait at least fifteen minutes before you do it again. You will probably want to do this no more than twice a day.

Another way to work with this tone is to chant it silently, as an ongoing tone at almost any time *except* when you are doing something that requires your complete attention, like driving or operating machinery. These are spiritual practices that take your awareness away from this world. For your and other's safety, do not do them when you need to pay attention here. Chanting the HU in this way can help center you and bring you into balance.

Remember to ground yourself by doing the "E" as described earlier, drinking some water, and stretching a little when you are done.

ANI-HU

"Ani-Hu" is a variation of the "HU," with the added dimension of bringing in the quality of empathy with others. As you chant this tone, you may find that quality of empathy increasing. To chant this out loud, you would say, "Ani-Hu," as you breathe out. It would sound like, "Aaaniiiii Huuuuuuu." If you are chanting silently, you might chant "Ani" as you breathe in and "Hu" as you breathe out.

You may find yourself doing it one way today and the other way tomorrow. These tones are given to you with flexibility in how you work with them. Do what works best for you.

While you are chanting, focus your attention on an imaginary spot near the very center of your head. If you were to draw an imaginary line from the spot between your eyes to the back of your head, and another from the top of one ear to the other, the place where those lines intersect is where you want to focus. This is where the energy of the Soul gathers.

Chant the tone you have chosen, either the HU or the Ani-Hu, for about five minutes. It doesn't matter if you chant silently or out loud. There is no rush. It is helpful to chant in sync with your breath. After chanting for about five minutes, stop, and just listen. Then, after five minutes, you can chant again, or get up, get grounded, and go on with your day.

What you experience during and after doing spiritual exercises is very individual. You may see colors; you may feel spiritual energy come in as warmth, or as a tingling in your hands, feet, or head. You may feel as though your body is changing shape or size, or getting very light—or heavy. Your vision might get a little blurry. These shifts indicate that your consciousness is moving within you. Don't be concerned; they're steps in your progression into Spirit.

Bringing spiritual frequencies into your body can push out negativity that you've stored or hidden in your consciousness. Your mind may wander. Memories of things you haven't thought of for a long time

may come up. Feelings may surface from seemingly
nowhere. You might suddenly feel like crying. Your
mind might take off into lists of things to do, wor-
ries, or concerns. You are learning to simply observe,
let things go, and keep on chanting. Some of those
thoughts or feelings may have been locked away in
your consciousness for a long time and are being
cleared out by the Light. There's no need to be concerned; let these things go into the Light. You don't
need them. Your focus is on observing and listening.
It's your opportunity to clear yourself and move one
step closer to your spiritual reality.

Some people can't sleep after doing spiritual exercises. If this happens, you'll know it's better to do
them in the morning, or certainly not just before bed.
Other people experience deep, restful sleep after doing
spiritual exercises, so doing them at night would work
well for them. Explore, experiment, and see how these
things work for you. Although spiritual exercises are
designed for inner experiences, the results often spill
over into this world. You may find that you are calmer,
that things that used to disturb you don't bother you
as much. You may experience a sense of well-being,
of contentment and happiness. And sometimes, you
see more clearly what you need to do in your life to
handle things better.

Keeping a Journal

Writing down your experiences after doing spiritual exercises can help you capture your experiences
which, like dreams, may fade away from memory.

You might track the date and how long you did spiritual exercises, what chant you did and how you did it, and any experiences you had. This could be as simple as writing, "My mind wouldn't leave me alone. I kept thinking of all the things I have to do." Or maybe you saw a spot of color as you were sitting quietly and listening. Maybe you have some beautiful thoughts or awareness to write, or you have forgiven and released something that was bothering you, or you have a solution to some difficulty. This is another aspect of observing; track what your experience is, with no judgment of anything being too ordinary to write down...or so grand that you think every session from then on should be like that.

You might also write in your journal things you notice *after* doing se's. Maybe your dreams become more vivid, or you are calmer than usual, or you notice some other change in your life. Doing spiritual exercises is an exercise in awareness, and keeping a journal can help you capture what is happening. Find what works for you and use it.

If you would like to share these spiritual techniques with others, give them this book or *Inner Worlds of Meditation,* which includes many other meditations. Then they are responsible for reading all the information. If you teach spiritual exercises to others, then *you* are responsible for getting all the information to them accurately. This process of doing spiritual exercises is simple, but unless you are a spiritual teacher, there is a lot going on that you cannot perceive. So let someone else be the teacher. You can share the value you get from doing spiritual exercises, but let people get the instructions from this book so they can fully understand what they are doing.

As you explore and become more attuned to the Light, you become an ambassador of the Light. This does not mean that you proselytize. The way you live becomes your example, and through your example and the radiant energy that fills you through your spiritual practices, you "turn people on" to the Spirit and the Light. When people who have repeatedly taken drugs turn to the Light—really turn to it—there's no stopping them. It took a kind of courage to put drugs in their body and to go with that. They didn't know where they were going or whether they would come back; they didn't know what the experience was going to be. These people have nerve. They love adventure. They're not afraid to travel the realms of Light.

These people make good ambassadors of Light. They will go anyplace. They've already been judged, rejected, and misunderstood when they were doing drugs. They figure that if they're now doing things the right way, what difference does anyone's judgments make? They'll just keep moving on, and there's no stopping them.

When you are working with the Spirit, your responsibility is to hold the Light for others until they open up to it. It's best not to judge; you hold yourself back if you say, "Oh, look at those deadbeats; they're no good." You can hold the Light for them, educate them if they are open to it, and let them see the reality of their action. You can show them that they can go inside and get their spiritual fulfillment without taking a drug. You place the Light with them in loving neutrality. Someday, when they weaken for just a moment and say, "Oh God, I need help," the Light will flood them. They will realize their spiritual promise and their spiritual heritage as children of Light.

12

Your Spiritual Heritage

Don't depend on anything, but use every experience to step up. If you can use drugs to help you step up and then leave them alone, that's fine, but it's a risky, tricky path to choose. If you start depending on them, then you're hooked, and it's a downward spiral. You don't have to do drugs to get "up." You can go very high through the Spirit in a way that is far more fulfilling.

If you dent or scrape your car, you can get the damaged area repaired and painted, but it's never quite the same. People point it out: "Hey, you had your car painted there, didn't you?" You have to get a whole new paint job, and about that time you figure you might just as well get a new car. But it's kind of hard to get a new body or mind. In our society, psychiatrists are the ones who try to repair the damage. That takes hours and hours of therapy, and it's very expensive. And even then, you are never quite the same.

Experiences that damage the subconscious mind always leave their mark. When you turn to the Light, you get a real "overhaul" job. This can't be done by man. It must be through the action of the Spirit. Man can transplant hearts from one body to another, but nobody has been able to transplant a Soul or the Spirit. That's beyond the realm of man.

Ultimately, every one of us has a home in Spirit to return to. We are all here on earth to learn, to grow, and to complete whatever we have started. When you choose, as a Soul, to turn back into the Light and Sound that is your source, the inner strength to overcome the challenges, addictions, and limitations of this world comes into play. You begin to realize that the sensations of this world were all an attempt to remember and experience the immense loving Spirit from which you came.

Once you are touched by the Light and have a taste once again of your true nature, the thrills of this world become less compelling. It may sound difficult, impossible, or limiting to let go of alcohol, drugs, and other addictions. Yet the profound satisfaction you experience every time you touch to the Light more than replaces those things.

The path of knowing your own Soul, which we call Soul transcendence, is simple but not necessarily easy. This world is not eager to let you go and will tempt you to stay in illusion. Some of you may have a great deal of work to do to free yourself of the many levels on which addictions work. Know that you are never alone once you turn toward your spiritual home and begin to claim your divine heritage.

Glossary

Astral Realm. The psychic, material realm above the physical realm. The realm of the imagination. Intertwines with the physical as a vibratory rate.

Aura. The electromagnetic energy field that surrounds the human body. Has color and movement.

Basic self. One of three selves that make up physical consciousness. Has responsibility for bodily functions, maintains habits, maintains the psychic centers of the physical body. Handles communication from the conscious self (*see* **conscious self**) to the high self (*see* **high self**).

Chakras. Spiritual or metaphysical centers of the body, correlating to physical locations on the body. Each is a focus for the energy of a specific function.

Conscious self. One of three selves that make up physical consciousness. Handles life's daily decisions and actions. The self that makes conscious choices. It is the "captain of the ship" in that it can override both the basic self and the high self. The self that comes in as a tabula rasa. (*See also* **basic self** and **high self.**)

Etheric body. An exact replica of the physical body in every detail. Its purpose is to take on an illness before it reaches the physical body. Illness can often be removed from the etheric body double before it gets to the physical body. When a person is already ill physically, clearing the etheric body double, along with healing the physical body, can assist with healing.

High self. One of three selves that make up physical consciousness. Functions as one's spiritual guardian, directing the conscious self towards those experiences that are for one's greatest spiritual progression. (*See also* **basic self** and **conscious self.**)

Initiation. In the context of the Movement of Spiritual Inner Awareness (MSIA), it is the process of being connected to the Sound Current of God.

Karma. The law of cause and effect: as you sow, so shall you reap. The responsibility of each person for his or her actions. The law that directs and sometimes dominates a being's physical existence.

Levels of consciousness. Planes or realms of existence beyond the physical world, which correspond to the elements of human consciousness (imagination, mind, emotions, subconscious, unconscious, and Soul).

Light. The energy of Spirit that pervades all realms of consciousness.

Movement of Spiritual Inner Awareness (MSIA). An organization whose purpose is to teach Soul Transcendence, which is becoming aware of oneself as a Soul and as one with God, not as a theory but as a living reality. MSIA provides a variety of tools and techniques that allow people to experience their Soul and enhance their awareness of God.

Mystical Traveler Consciousness. An energy from the highest source of Light and Sound whose work in the world is Soul Transcendence and awakening people to an awareness of the Soul. This consciousness is always anchored on the planet through a physical form.

Soul. Essence of God in the physical body. The basic element of human existence, forever connected to God. The God within.

Soul Transcendence. To know yourself as a Soul and as one with God. This is done by transcending the lower levels—physical, astral (imagination), causal (emotions), mental (mind), and etheric (unconscious)—and moving into the Soul realm and above. It is the work of the Mystical Traveler.

Spiritual Exercises. The process of chanting the HU, the Ani-Hu, or one's initiatory tone. An active technique for bypassing the mind and emotions by chanting a tone to connect to the Sound Current. Assists a person in breaking through the illusions of the lower levels and eventually moving into awareness of the Soul consciousness and above.

Sound of God. Also known as the Sound current. The audible energy that flows from God through all realms. The spiritual energy on which a person returns to the heart of God.

Spirit. The essence of creation. Infinite and eternal.

Resources

Further Exploration

John-Roger's teachings are found in a rich variety of materials. The following is a brief list of resources to support you in your further exploration of Soul Transcendence. You will find more at www.msia.org.

Books by John-Roger

When Are You Coming Home?
A Personal Guide To Soul Transcendence
(written with Pauli Sanderson, DSS)

How did John-Roger attain awareness of who he truly is? He approached life like a scientist in a laboratory. He found methods for integrating the sacred with the mundane, the practical with the mystical. He noted what worked and what didn't. In his story you will find practical keys for making your own life work better and for attuning to the source of wisdom that is always within you. Perhaps this is the greatest key that John-Roger found on his journey: that everything in life brings opportunities for upliftment, learning and growth. From his life you can discover how to make every day propel you further on your exciting adventure home. Includes a meditation CD through the inner realms of Spirit.

ISBN 1893020231, Hardbound, $19.95

Momentum: Letting Love Lead
Simple Practices for Spiritual Living
(written with Paul Kaye, DSS)

With simplicity, this book communicates a profound message: You can live a fulfilling life, not by trying harder, working more, or sleeping less, but by letting love lead you.

ISBN 1893020185, Hardbound, $19.95

Inner Worlds of Meditation

John-Roger describes the process of meditation and the inner realms of consciousness that can be reached by going within. With practical guidance through a number of meditation techniques, this book is a guide to your inner worlds of meditation.

ISBN 0-914829-45-9, Paperback, $12
Also available as a 3-CD set, ISBN 0-914829-64-5, $30

Spiritual Warrior: The Art of Spiritual Living

An essential book for every person who wants to integrate his or her spiritual and material lives and live successfully within both. A practical guide to finding greater meaning in everyday life, this revolutionary approach puts us firmly on the higher road to greater health, wealth, and happiness; prosperity, abundance, and riches; loving, caring, and sharing; and touching to others with the overflow of all of this.

ISBN 0-914829-36-X, Hardbound, $20

Audio/Video Materials by John-Roger
Healing Through Inner Peace

John-Roger shows the importance of moving toward the solution instead of focusing on the problem. In the process, he presents techniques for healing the kinds of emotional hurts that are behind all sorts of expressions of violence.

Available from MSIA audio tape, #7703, $10
videotape #VC-7703, $20

Words of Comfort for Challenging Times

Is something in your world upsetting you? When your world rocks, the eleven excerpts in this CD will remind you of what is really true. Take a moment to listen to them as you feel challenged. You'll be reassured that God has a purpose for everything, even though we sometimes can't see it.

Available from MSIA Compact disk, #7827-CD, $15

Turning Points to Personal Liberation

The six audiotapes in this packet provide direct, insightful information regarding the causes and cures for hurt, anger, confusion, jealousy, severe mood swings, insecurity, and loneliness. They deliver practical keys for gaining greater acceptance, healing, understanding, loving, freedom, and liberation.

Topics include: Keys to handling negative emotions; turning hurt and anger to acceptance and loving; five characteristics and cures of emotional mood swings; ten of life's essential questions; insecurity and what to do about it; healing the hurt.

Available from MSIA
6 audiotape packet, #3916, $45

Soul Journey through Spiritual Exercises
Three tapes and a booklet, including a spiritual exercises seminar, "Meditation for Soul Travel," and "HU Chant & Breathing Exercise," all conducted by John-Roger. You are your Soul. There is no more important mission than awakening to your divine inheritance. The Soul Journey packet facilitates the trip.

Available from MSIA
3 audio cassettes, #3718, $25

Soul Awareness Discourses
Soul Awareness Discourses
A Course in Soul Transcendence
Year One

Soul Awareness Discourses are designed to teach Soul Transcendence: becoming aware of yourself as a Soul and as one with God. They are for people who want a consistent, time-proven approach to their spiritual unfoldment.

The first year Discourse Kit includes 12 individual Discourses (one for each month of the year), a deluxe binder, a beautiful storage case, and resource material for tracking your spiritual growth and awareness. Topics include Realms of Light, Acceptance, The Law of Cause and Effect, Responsibility, and more.

Studying Discourses often leads to better health, greater wealth, more loving relationships, and knowing God as a living reality in your life.

Discourses come with a full, no-questions-asked, money-back guarantee. If at any time you decide this course of study is not right for you, return them and you will promptly receive a full refund.

Available from MSIA
$50/Year One (12 booklets), #5000

Books are available at your local bookstore, and all books, tapes and CD's are available at:

MSIA
P.O. Box 513935
Los Angeles, CA 90051
(323) 737-4055
www.msia.org

Other services available through MSIA

Loving Each Day—Free Daily E-mail Subscription

A daily e-mail message to inspire and lift your Spirit.

Available in four languages: English, Spanish, French, and Portuguese. For a free subscription, visit www.lovingeachday.org.

Loving Each Day e-postcards are also available at www.lovingeachday.org.

Aura Balances, Polarity Balances, Innerphasings

Aura balances clear the aura, or energy field, that surrounds the body. They are offered in a series of three, with touch-ups after the series is completed. This technique, as done through MSIA, can clear the residuals of drugs and alcohol from the aura and help bring the body, mind, and emotions into a greater creative flow. With a more clear perception of yourself and your world, you can also be more available to Spirit in your life.

A *polarity balance* enhances the flow of energy within your body and brings the vibratory frequencies of the body into greater balance. The effects of releasing blocks in your body can include more energy, a sense of lightness as though a weight has been lifted, an increased sense of well-being, and a greater ability to function physically in the world.

An *innerphasing* is an audiotaped session created to specifically address areas in yourself you wish to change. You listen to this tape for at least 32 days in row, at least once per day. An innerphasing can help make changes in the unconscious, where blocks that can be difficult to handle often reside.

For more information about these services, including costs and how to make appointments, contact MSIA at (323) 737-4055.

About the Authors

John-Roger, D.S.S.

A teacher and lecturer of international stature, John-Roger is an inspiration in the lives of many people around the world. For over three decades, his wisdom, humor, common sense, and love have helped people to discover the Spirit within themselves and find health, peace, and prosperity.

With two co-authored books on the *New York Times* Best-Seller List to his credit, and more than three dozen self-help books and audio albums, John-Roger offers extraordinary insights on a wide range of topics. He is the founder of the nondenominational Church of the Movement of Spiritual Inner Awareness (MSIA), which focuses on Soul Transcendence; founder and Chancellor of the University of Santa Monica; founder and President of Peace Theological

Seminary & College of Philosophy; founder of Insight Seminars; and founder and President of the Institute for Individual and World Peace.

John-Roger has given over 5,000 lectures and seminars worldwide, many of which are televised nationally on his cable program, "That Which Is," through the Network of Wisdoms. He has been a featured guest on "Larry King Live," "Politically Incorrect," "The Roseanne Show," and appears regularly on radio and television.

An educator and minister by profession, John-Roger continues to transform lives by educating people in the wisdom of the spiritual heart. For more information about John-Roger, visit: www.john-roger.org

Michael McBay, M.D.

Michael McBay was born in 1955 in Atlanta. His parents were prominent academic professors in chemistry and mathematics. After receiving an academic scholarship, Michael integrated Atlanta's last private white High School during the 60's and experienced first-hand the discrimination characteristic of the integration years in the South. Michael McBay attended Stanford University, UCLA Medical School, and entered Emergency Medicine Residency at King/Drew Medical Center in Los Angeles, all the while performing original music in rock clubs at night. It was in connection with his performance activities that he became addicted to crack cocaine, which resulted in the loss of almost everything he had worked for, including his medical license.

With the help of God, John-Roger, his mother, martial arts, and a few close friends, Michael overcame his drug addiction and has completely reinstated his life as well as his medical license and practice. As part of his recovery, he endeavors to assist other recovering persons and physicians. This book is a natural extension of this endeavor.

Mandeville Press
www.mandevillepress.org
jrbooks@mandevillepress.org

MSIA
P.O. Box 513935
Los Angeles, CA 90051-1935
(323) 737-4055
soul@msia.org
http://www.msia.org

Printed in the United States
38169LVS00002BB/1-249